2008

I0485100

Skinny Finance for a Customer-Centered Educational Administration

Jon C. Stephens, MBA, Ed. D.

SKINNY FINANCE

Skinny Finance is a new culture of educational business services that is robust and rigorous in its creation, evaluation and analysis of financial systems but is gentle on people. It is marked by excellent customer service for the other departments of the institution. It moves the financial review processes from one of transaction-based analysis to a system wide approach. Visit www.SkinnyAdmin.com for more information. To order more copies, please shop: www.BookSurge.com.

Table of Contents

ii *Table of Contents*

What is Skinny Finance?

"Skinny Finance" refers to an approach of institutional
finance and business services that emphasizes customer
service, elimination of unnecessary tasks and automation of
routine tasks within a financial control environment. It is also
marked by a return of budget control to the budget managers. It
is called "Skinny" because it creates an atmosphere in which the
functions of the Finance Department are "Skinny" with respect to
their impact on program managers. The instructional services
conduct business in the institution with very little impact and
influence from the organization's Department of Finance. It is a
program that is rigorous on systems and gentle on people.

Have you had the feeling that "you cannot fight city hall?"
In your organization, is the Department of Finance that
monolithic governing body that seems to stop your business

activity with every small variation in transactions? Does it always seem that "the auditor said..." and you are barred from completing your business? These are signs that your Finance Department needs a new skinny culture.

The heart of Skinny Finance is that a transformed Department of Finance concentrates its education, experience, talents and time on perfecting the systems by which services are delivered to the end users and they step back from the transactional analysis that tends to slow the institution's business. There will always be a system of checks and balances provided by the leadership of the Department of Finance but those systems can be established to routinely process transactions without the excruciating level of review offered by the traditional transaction-based finance.

Do you want to simply order a book? Do you want to have your book delivered quickly without endless layers of pre-approval, approval and Über-approval? Then Skinny Finance is a culture you will want to evaluate.

Skinny Finance borrows from the lessons learned by the author throughout his educational administrative career, backed with research. One of the professional disciplines learned along

the way and incorporated into this new financial culture is Lean

Construction Scheduling.

> "The goals of lean thinking redefine performance
> against three dimensions of perfection: (1) a
> uniquely custom product, (2) delivered instantly,
> with (3) nothing in stores. This is an ideal that
> maximizes value and minimizes waste. The goals
> demand a new way to coordinate action, one that
> is applicable to industries far removed from
> manufacturing." (Howell and Ballard, 1998)

This skinny book about Skinny Finance is a quick start to

planning for a new culture of end product business services

delivery without requiring the budget managers to also be

finance experts. This new culture assumes that budget

managers know how to best operate a department and that

finance knows how best to establish the systems by which

services are delivered to the operating departments.

The Point: Skinny Finance breaks the log jams that often

slow educational administration to an excruciating crawl.

Part One – The Origin of Skinny Finance

Patriot Games

She walked into my office and tossed a file on my desk. "Check this out," said the Purchasing Director as I reached for the manila file folder. "This is classic." I quickly recognized the purchase requisition form inside. They are used by the schools in our district to make purchases of supplies and materials. There was a shiny advertisement for a wall clock, printed with the school name, "Orange Glen High School" and an image of their mascot, The Patriot.

For a limited time only, the principal of the school could receive a clock with the school name and mascot for only one dollar. Wow, what a deal! One dollar. It was an introductory offer that, I am sure, the vendor made to help promote sales to students, faculty and staff at the full retail price. There is nothing

wrong with that. A California public school can certainly

purchase a clock for one dollar.

I was the Director of Finance and in charge of making

sure that all purchases, no matter how small, are made

"appropriately." There must be safeguards against misuse of

funds and, according to the Governmental Accounting

Standards Board, I need to take a fixed asset inventory. Would

the one dollar clock be in the inventory? Would we pay for it

using a standard commercial warrant drawn on the Treasury of

the County of San Diego? Could we write a revolving cash

check?

All of these issues whisked through my head but I knew

what the Director of Purchasing was saying: "Isn't it funny that

we are writing a purchase order for one dollar." And on a

different day, I may have responded in a different way. But on

this day I was not in my normal mood. I was feeling feisty. I had

just finished a study of the cost of administration for a

proposition on the California Ballot, the 95 / 5 Initiative. The

proposition would have required California public schools to spend 95% of its general unrestricted funds on activities in the classroom. They could spend only 5% on administrative services.

When I had concluded the study, I learned that our district did not spend anywhere near five percent of its budget outside of the classroom. (Stephens, 1998) The perception among voters, however, was that administrative expenditures accounted for more than 5% of general fund expenditures. This was a perfect example of how the voters needed education to understand (Johnson, 1998) that many of our school administrations were then already lean and needed no legal requirements to force compliance.

So I learned that our school district was compliant with the 95 / 5 Initiative. But I had also learned other things. My study revealed that it costs $176 to process the average purchase order. The finance staff spent over $200 processing invoices when they arrived and it took more than fifteen days to place an order from the time it was received in finance. Orange Glen's purchase request for one dollar was laying conspicuously close to my administrative cost report.

I opened my wallet, took out a dollar bill and put it in the postage paid envelope. "There," I said, "we just saved the taxpayers close to $400. My colleague was stunned. "You can't do that. We need to place the order," she said. I replied, "I just did place the order." To punctuate how I felt, I walked the envelope to the mail room and dropped it in the bin. It was done.

Well, it was not done for the Director of Purchasing and, as it turned out, it was not done for me either. My colleague went to the Superintendent of schools. She protested my defiance of the very financial control procedures that I set up. The rules were my responsibility to enforce and monitor. There were drama filled moments when I met with the Superintendent and the Director of Purchasing. And I got the expected response from the Superintendent, "follow the finance procedures." But after my colleague left, I was called back into the Superintendent's office and we had a long chat about the theory behind my "saving the taxpayers almost $400."

Was the savings real? Or was it just an accounting shell game? I reasoned that, in the long run, a more efficient Finance Department would save money, time and aggravation. If I wanted to change to a culture that would "just put a dollar in the

envelope" (so to speak) I would need to change the way we

operated the Department of Finance. I would need to develop a

new culture that was smarter; it would look past the individual

tasks and focus on the big picture of finance. The new

department policies would need to be more elegant, focused on

Strategic Goals and have less of an impact on the business of

the educational programs. It would be leaner. I wanted "Skinny

Finance."

The Point: Skinny finance needs to focus on the big picture

and not be tied so tightly to the rules of transactions that it loses

all logic. The school district really saved $400 and I don't care

what my fellow administrator thinks.

Kokanee Accounting

I eventually left that school district and moved my family to beautiful Lake Tahoe, California. I was the new Vice President of business services for Lake Tahoe Community College. Initially I moved to Lake Tahoe to ski and enjoy the outdoors but I quickly fell in love with the college, its mission and the students, faculty and staff. They were the Kokanees, the only educational institution I have worked for that has a trout for a mascot. And it is a cool trout.

Starting my job in February, I was immediately thrust into the budget development process. After all there were only four months until the end of the fiscal year, June 30. In a cabinet meeting a Dean was discussing her preparations for the end of the fiscal year. I wondered why she cared or even knew about the end of the fiscal year. In my world of Skinny Finance, there is no end of the year; time just marches on. College business just marches on. This Dean gave me sage advice, "spend your entire budget now or you will be locked out." Wow, I just arrived at the college and already I am under imminent threat of the dreaded "lock out."

Not being one who is afraid to admit what he does not know, I asked, "What is lock out?" The Dean's response was serious, efficient and to the point. "The Director of Fiscal Services puts out a memo every year about this time that says all purchasing must stop for the end of the fiscal year." The end of the fiscal year? That isn't for another four months. Are we really shutting down the business of the college when the year is barely half over? Does this mean the students go home? "We are not shutting down business services just because we are nearing the end of the year," I replied. The Dean was stunned. "Oh, you better check with Fiscal Services about that," she warned.

So I did check with Fiscal Services. And they confirmed that they prefer to shut down early so that they have time to receive shipments and pay invoices before the end of the fiscal year churns by. This Director of Fiscal Services is a smart, enthusiastic, well-respected person. She would never make up a false deadline simply to make her job easier. There are good reasons for asking budget managers to expend their budgets in a timely manner.

First of all, there really is a lot of work to do at the end of the year and it is a good time for the finance staff to be freed up for those activities. There is the argument that if goods or services are not received by June 30, then the expenditure must be recorded in the subsequent year. There are special cases for categorically funded programs that must spend their funds in a given year. A prudent Director of Fiscal Services will also say that we want all expenditures completed so we can accurately project the ending fund balance. Too many times, campus constituencies accuse Fiscal Services of intentionally underestimating the ending fund balance to boost funds available for the next year and make the current year fund balances look good. In most cases, however, the unspent discretionary budgets are more to blame than an overly-cautious Director of Finance for unexpectedly high ending fund balances.

But the most compelling argument for encouraging that expenditures be made throughout the year and not all at the end of the year is: general fund revenue is generated for the current students' benefit. If funds are generated currently, they should be spent to benefit the current students. OK, I understand that capital outlay and other non-general funds are special cases. But for the most part, the best reason to encourage faculty and staff to spend their budgets evenly throughout the year is to benefit the students evenly throughout the year. Under a Skinny Finance program, the closing out of financial activities will be based upon the benefit to the students, not the convenience of the skinny finance staff.

A skinnier approach to the problem of expenditures made close to the end of the fiscal year would be to analyze the system that produces the close-out entries and to fully develop the connection of expenditures to Strategic Goals, discussed later. To support on-going Strategic Goals of the institution, the Department of Finance may develop a system by which account balances are automatically rolled (Li, 2003) to the next year if the expenditure will continue in pursuit of the Strategic Goals. If the expenditure plan does not support the Strategic Goals, then the appropriation must stop for that reason alone. The function of the calendar changing cannot be the impetus for budget

transactions, under Skinny Finance.

The point: A Skinny Finance never shuts down. It performs

all year round.

Water Water Everywhere

Carrying over from my previous administrative position at Escondido Union High School District, I wanted something new and refreshing for Lake Tahoe Community College. What, if anything, could my Skinny Finance bring to the end of a fiscal year for this college?

Money to the instructional programs is like water to a farm. We can grow wheat, corn, soy beans or rice but they all need water. If we deny water to any one of our "crops" then we will lose the harvest. If we deny funds to any of our instructional programs we will lose the programs and our instructional goals will not be met. So the question for my Skinny Finance is: "Can we stop watering the crop when we near the end of the fiscal year?" No. They will die.

As I explained it to my Fiscal Services Department, the business we conduct at the college is like a river, it keeps flowing. It slows in the summer and runs harder in the winter, but the river keeps flowing. Previously the college was treating the

17

business services like a lake that fills up in the winter and spring and then dries up in the summer. This is simply not the case. What if I called our health benefits provider and told them, "the college is closed for business, we will pay our premiums in the fall." I doubt we would have health care for long. And I doubt I would have a job for long.

Skinny Finance plans for continuous operations. Sure there are well-reasoned arguments for cut-off dates, beyond which expenditures may be recorded in the subsequent fiscal year but, for the most part, our department must plan to provide services all year round. Skinny Finance analyzes the business systems rigorously and develops paths for the water to flow. We channel water to this activity and that activity but we never stop it.

Under Skinny Finance, the real work comes in the beginning of the budget development process when we look at what "crops" to water and which will be plowed under to make way for new crops. When I worked at MiraCosta College, we had a significant budget shortfall due to a housing recession and the subsequent decrease in property taxes. We could not continue all programs.

Budget challenges like this are tough and call for hard decisions. But they are also the best opportunity to re-evaluate what we are doing as a college and redefine our mission. MiraCosta College had a large and successful manual drafting program. It was preparing students for jobs in engineering professions and in fields of design. Over the years preceding this housing recession, however, enrollment had dropped precipitously. What was happening? Well, the microcomputer age was firmly taking grip of the instruction and was changing the way students wanted to learn. Rather than holding a pencil and a drafting T, students wanted to learn Computer-Aided Drafting (CAD). And sure enough, the enrollment in those classes was booming.

The challenge for Skinny Finance then, is to learn from the Instructional Services Division which crop to water. We didn't have enough "water" for both drafting and CAD. The decision was clear but in the campus culture, it was difficult to change the course of that stream of water. The budget shortfall was an excellent catalyst for change but my department needed

direction from instructional services and from the campus

community as a whole. The college needed a compelling reason

to shut off the water and channel it to the other program, CAD.

The Strategic Goals and Objectives are the best friends

to Skinny Finance. Sure enough, the Board, upon

recommendation from the campus constituencies, had adopted

a goal that required the college to develop new and emerging

technologies to benefit the students. Bingo. My Skinny Finance

then had the catalyst (budget shortfall) and the mission

(Strategic Goal) to implement a channel diversion away from

manual drafting and toward CAD. And sure enough, instructional

services gave finance direction, using the Strategic Plan as a

blueprint. We changed crops. I won't deceive you. There were

hurt feelings and the culture of the college resisted the change

at first. But when the faculty saw the benefits of the change to

the students, the Academic Senate was supportive of the budget

change.

And this brings up another point about Skinny Finance.

We do not lead change in instructional programs. That is the job of the Academic Senate, the faculty and the Instructional

Administration. But we can certainly link expenditures to the

Strategic Goals and identify where we seem to be on target and

where we might suggest re-channeling of funds.

The point: Funds to an instructional program are like water

to a crop. We will lose our harvest if we simply cut off the supply.

The Lamplighter

I walked into my new office at Escondido Union High School District. My predecessor had a big, comfortable leather chair that sat imposing with its high-back and well-stuffed arm rests. "This is not going to do," I thought. The Director of Finance cannot be seen sitting in a chair that cost more than the annual supply budget for most teachers. The chair was history. I don't know where it went or how it got there but I never saw the chair again.

So I was sitting in my replacement chair, a reasonably priced, comfortable chair that said to my clients, "I will not put my wants before the needs of the students." Did people really look at the former, big leather chair and think that I could have used the money for the students? I did not really care. When I saw the chair that is what I thought. In my new chair, reading my predecessor's budget manual, I heard a meek voice interrupt me. "Mr. Stephens, I just wanted to introduce myself. I am one of your accounting technicians." She was a young woman who was clearly nervous. I later found out that my predecessor relished the fact that his staff feared him.

"Come in and sit down." She did so but with her hands firmly folded dutifully in her lap. She was in a closed stance. If meta-communication represents the majority of conversational content, she was closed and fearful. I asked her about herself. She started with a résumé-like recital and then described her typical areas of responsibilities for the school district. "But what about you?" I asked. "What do you want to do in the district?" It was obviously the first time anyone had ever asked her about what she wanted. She didn't say much. She just wanted to do a good job. I translated that to mean: "I don't want to be fired so I will work just hard enough to keep my job."

Over those first few weeks on this job, I learned that this young accounting technician, Theresa, was very bright, was well-liked and had a wry sense of humor. Unfortunately, she did not feel comfortable demonstrating any of her personal qualities in front of me. I later found out that my predecessor was so over-bearing and mean that nobody felt comfortable speaking to him and by a transitive property, I inherited the perception that one cannot just talk to the Director of Finance.

As is often the case in public education, resources were scarce and we needed to save wherever we could. I began a subtle campaign to identify redundant work, inefficiencies and unnecessary tasks. In my mind I was hunting for that leaner, Skinny Finance. I walked up to Theresa's desk. She had five piles of papers, receipts, travel requests and reports on her desk. There were five. She was hurried and my walking up made her appear even more nervous. "Hi Theresa," I said. "What are you working on?"

She stopped work and her shoulders slumped forward. "I am preparing your Board report," she answered. "I already wrote my report. It is done," I said. Theresa went on to explain that each month she gathers all of the receipts, purchase requests, travel requests and summarizes and totals them by Board member. There are five Board Members; there are five piles.

I asked her, "Do you do this every month?"

"Yes. Why?" then she replied. Many years prior, the Director of Finance sat in a contentious Board meeting. Two members were up for re-election and each was sniping at the other. One accused the other of frivolously spending school district money on boondoggles. When asked about the exact amount spent by each Board member, the Director of Finance did not know. And that is why, six years later, my well-paid accounting technician was compiling travel and expense data for each Board member before each Board meeting. "Since then, has the Board ever asked about the expenses?" I asked Theresa. She didn't know. "How long does it take you to compile?" I asked. "There are not a lot of Board expenses so the compilation is quick. But it takes me about twenty hours to review all of the financial activity to make sure I got everything."

Wow! Twenty hours a month down the drain. We needed to be skinnier than that. I told her to stop and not do this report again unless I asked her to do it. "What if the Board asks for it again?" she protested mildly. I could tell she would love to stop the tedious work. "If the Board asks, then I will tell them that it costs the school district twenty hours of accounting time to develop the report each month. If it is worth the twenty hours, then we will resume the report."

The entire time I worked for this school district, I was never asked about that report.

🖱 The point: Skinny finance cannot accommodate reports that continue indefinitely without periodic review of the report's value.

Ticket to Ride

Frances came into my office at Lake Tahoe Community College. She was interrupting me while I was in deep thought and writing a Board report. I was going through the annual ritual of finding a new way to present dry budget data. I don't think anyone looked forward all year to the budget presentation. It is long, tedious at times, yet important for the Board to see the data. After my first year at the college, I started summarizing the budget so that rather than reviewing each program budget, we would look at a macro level, at the changes in the budgets. We would look at the budget summarized at the Strategic Plan level. It was a small step toward a more logical budget but I was still not able to turn sterile data into a flashy fun report that really communicates the budget.

So while I sat there trying to force the round peg into the square hole, Frances interrupted my deep thought. "There is a student here to see you," she said to me. I was Vice President of

Business Services; students rarely come to see me and when they do, I make a point to give them my undivided attention. But I was in the middle of budget. I scowled at Frances indicating how busy I was. "You should really see him," she continued. Frances knew better than I did. I need to always make time for students but this was coming at an inconvenient time. I was to present the budget the next week and I really needed to study it. Frances let the student in.

When I teach as an adjunct faculty member, I see students regularly. The encounters are very enjoyable. I love to understand how the students view my class, how it fits into their lives and how they view the world. There is something truly refreshing about their youthful optimism. I think secretly I want to share in that optimism but as life's stresses press inward, I tend to lose my optimism. So I changed my mindset to welcome the student and make time for him. I introduced myself.

This student started in a very animated and flustered manner. My staff had ticketed his motorcycle for parking incorrectly and, in the process, my staff had scratched the new paint on his gas tank, where they taped the parking ticket. He was angry. As I listened to him, I tried to remain patient. But I was not patient. I was impatient. And I had not changed my mindset at all. All I had done was prepare for a delightful student conversation. And this was not delightful. "I don't have time for this," I thought to myself. "I am preparing a budget for the Board to consider. I don't have time for a scratched gas tank."

What an arrogant, ignorant thought I had. Fortunately I only said apologetic comments aloud. But my mind was focusing on how insensitive and uncaring my thoughts were. Here this young man comes to my office because he loves his motorcycle and is proud of his new purchase. He feels my staff scratched it. How could I not care for him and his feelings? How did I get to the point that a document is more important than the students we serve? This is craziness.

I offered the student a bottle of water and we sat and talked. And I really paid attention to him. I focused on his feelings and what he was telling me with his body language. This man was really hurting. After I listened, I asked if he could show me the bike. He was proud to do so. I walked out with him. We were talking about his roommate and how he was on his own for the first time. He was struggling financially but making it. And he was focusing on his future. He was the ideal student who benefits so much from our instructional programs.

When we got to the bike, I asked him to show me the bike. He pointed to the scratch. I asked him again, "Seriously, show me your motorcycle." He hopped on the bike and started to show me the controls and the gages. He was proud of his bike. I was excited to see how happy he was with this first major purchase in his young life. Then I looked at the scratch. It was a small piece of crusted pine sap from an overhead tree. I flicked it with my finger and it flew off the gas tank. It sure did look like a scratch. The student turned red. "I am so embarrassed," he said. "I thought it was scratched." It wasn't. But I thanked the young man for showing me his bike.

I thought a lot about the encounter. To this day, I cannot explain how I was so filled with self-importance that I was willing to work on my budget while this student suffered from the scratch. And I didn't care when he first came into my office. Was my work so damned important that I could not take a few minutes to get to know a student and help him with his problem?

Thank God Frances didn't let me get away with that attitude on that day. She insisted that I meet with the student.

Much later, as I sat considering Skinny Finance, I am drawn back to that chance encounter. How does a piece of crusted pine sap impact Skinny Finance? For me, the impact is that I need to stay mission-focused, student-focused. At the moment that student came to my office, did I really have anything more important than to listen to him? Was the budget that important? Was I that important? I had my shot as an undergraduate and I had faculty and administrators help me. Yet many years later, when I was Vice President of this college, I was unwilling to help this student when he first came to my office. I now realize that I was in a transaction-based analysis of the budget and I was off the mission of the college. We are here to serve students, not to tolerate them or avoid meeting with them. Skinny Finance needs to focus on mission, not on details of a budget document. Sure the details need to be completed but the budget is worthless without a strong mission to which I can ascribe.

The Point: Administrators of Skinny Finance need to personally focus on the mission of the educational institution. It will build character and create an atmosphere in which everything we do is mission-centric, student-centric.

Part Two – Symptoms of Chubby Finance

Learning to Fly

While an administrator at MiraCosta College, I felt a bit disconnected to the primary mission of the college. We were in the business of providing futures to our students and I did not feel like my efforts in finance were mission-centric.

Some might say that the college sells education to students, but I disagree. We provide education but we are really selling a brighter, more productive and fulfilling future. That is an aggressive and ambitious goal. Are we really responsible to ensure that a student has a big house, two cars, a plasma television and annual trips to the Caribbean? No. But through our excellent faculty our students can reach their goals. We provide the environment in which a student can learn and the students have the choice to learn. In my mind, this is the difference between the teaching environment and the learning environment. I prefer the latter. Believe me, when I earned my doctorate, the faculty was not teaching; they made tools available and I chose to learn.

So there I was, the Director in charge of this large finance department in a role to support instruction but not actually delivering instruction to our students. The best administrator I have ever worked with is Guy Lease. He is an intelligent, charismatic man with a true heart for delivering the best education he can. He is a great leader. And he was also the President of Lake Tahoe Community College. He plans to retire this year. He will be missed.

Guy told me that in a previous career, he worked with the Air Force. "In the Air Force," he explained, "there are pilots and there is everyone else who keep the planes in the air. In business services at the college, we keep the planes in the air. But we are not the pilots, the faculty is."

Well, I was at MiraCosta College, several years away from meeting Guy Lease and I was several years away from hearing that insightful thought about the airplanes. I just knew that I was not flying the airplane like the faculty was. And I knew I had something to offer the students. Computer and Information Science. This is an easy call. I have minimum qualifications in several faculty service areas but I knew I wanted to teach Computer Studies.

I made an appointment with Jill Malone, the Chair of the Computer and Information Science Department. Jill is a cheery, intelligent, humorous woman with a lot of experience teaching. Jill and I met for just a few minutes. She had previously looked over my curricula vitae and was happy to welcome me into her department as an adjunct faculty member. Wonderful! I am getting my chance to fly. I would directly touch the lives of the students. And I was impressed that Jill had the authority and was empowered to hire me on the spot. I thought, "It takes an Act of Congress for the Director of Finance to hire someone."

Over the next few weeks, I was bombarded with paperwork for my new adjunct position. There were hire papers, finger prints, tuberculosis tests, workplace harassment notifications, I-9, W-4, blood borne pathogens. I received seventeen pages of hire papers to teach one four unit class. And since I was already an administrator, didn't the college already have my fingerprints, tuberculosis test, I-9, W-4 and the like? What was going on?

After receiving this stack of documents, I was planning to go back to work and find out which department was so hungry for paper that it requires seventeen pages to hire one adjunct faculty member. Sadly, I learned, one of the offending departments was my own. I had recently assumed responsibility for the Payroll Department but not Human Resources. Between the two of them, they managed to send me seventeen pages of hire documents. I was asked for my nearest relative contact information three times. There had to be a better way.

During the hire process I kept notes of how many phones calls, letters, flyers and forms I received. It was incredible. I suddenly understood what the Academic Senate had been saying about difficulties hiring and retaining adjuncts. There are many issues involved in recruiting and retaining the faculty and they are not all centered in finance. But I clearly understood that some of the responsibility was sadly mine.

I met with the Payroll staff. They did not like the burdensome volume of paper that flowed across their desks and filled their filing cabinets to bulging. They just had no way out. A new law passes about "Blood Borne Pathogens" and, boom, we have a new form. So I asked the staff to shut down for a mini-retreat. My Accounting staff filled in for a day while the Payroll staff and I met and talked about what we were doing. We compared notes regarding what paper processed across which desks. Would you be surprised if you found out that two different people were sending out essentially the same notice to new hires? And how does this continue unabated? Well, what newly hired employee wants to walk into the Payroll Department and declare the emperor has no clothes? Who will complain about paperwork right after being hired? Since I was already an administrator, I was that person who pointed out the redundancy.

"Three," Debbie from Payroll told me. "We can get our paperwork down to three pages." That is what I like to hear. The business of the college just got skinnier.

The Point: Skinny finance relies upon frequent, critical analysis of workflow to avoid duplication of effort.

Simon Says

"We need to hire another budget analyst," I was told by the Budget Supervisor.

"OK, what would that new person do?" I replied. Vivian went on to explain that the number of budget transactions crossing her desk was burdensome and she could not keep up. I had many thoughts but the first thing I wanted to know was, why now? What precipitated this need for new staff? Vivian went on to explain what the auditor conveyed. Vivian said, "I will be subject to more mistakes if I continue to work alone on budget entries to the financial control system (FCS)." I asked her which auditor made the comment because I wanted to explore options to the comment. "It was Simon," Vivian continued. "He told me that coding the budget entries is taking so long that I need help." OK, I can be a bit of a smart ass, so I had to say it. "Simon says, 'we need another budget analyst'."

All joking aside, budget transaction errors can cause serious difficulties in the Finance Department. Whether the solution was more staff or a different process, I needed to find help for Vivian. We started by discussing why we had so many budget transactions. Well, it was a large budget, there are many school sites and many of the transactions coming across Vivian's desk were incorrectly coded. I asked, "Do most budget managers get it right?" Vivian explained that the experienced budget managers usually get the account codes correct and know how to make a purchase. But the new managers tend to make frequent account coding errors. So, do we hire a new budget analyst because Vivian is so busy with the repetitious work of correcting account code errors? Or do we hire a new analyst because Simon Says?

If we could reduce the number of errant transactions to the level that Vivian did not spend all her day correcting them, then maybe my Budget Supervisor could be freed up to analyze the budget and the budget development process. But how could we manage a large budget for a large multi-site district without correcting endless errors? Since some managers correctly code and some do not, it would be very helpful if Vivian could train the new budget managers to work like the experienced managers. Maybe we could program some logic into the computer system so managers use a chart of accounts, already loaded into the FCS. This would prevent all coding errors.

Just by training, we put finance on a diet and we were getting skinnier. The next step was to build logic into the FCS that would make account code errors a thing of the past. The FCS is great for looking up valid codes and evaluating whether there is sufficient budget to purchase something. Our FCS was not a very effective tool for testing the appropriateness of expenditures – something I discuss later.

By simply educating the budget managers and building logic into the FCS, Vivian had fewer transactions to audit and correct. One might say, however, that the new process simply shifted the burden of the work to the budget managers and did not actually relieve the entire district of the workload. I believe it did relieve the total workload. When a budget manager selects an account from which a purchase will be made, it is just as easy to select a correct code as an incorrect code. But because the culture was built upon Vivian's final line of defense, the budget managers had little incentive to choose the correct code. Part of this culture was the cynical feeling that "no matter what we do, finance will end up changing it anyway." The challenge to change culture is a topic of discussion later.

When the FCS locks out incorrect account codes, the budget managers can easily find the correct account with sufficient budget to accommodate the expenditure. This is Skinny Finance. We lowered the impact of the finance staff upon the end users, the budget managers. In addition, we didn't follow Simon Says; we didn't need another budget analyst and much of Vivian's time was freed to analyze the budget and train new managers. At her level of expertise and training, this is the high level at which I would hope her to operate.

The Point: Look for signs that repeated errors are endlessly corrected in the Finance Department

.

If I Ran the Zoo

I credit Dr. Suess with many of the wonderful ideas I
have swimming around in my head since I was a child. *Horton
Hears a Who*, recently released in a movie, is a wonderful
lesson about caring for other people. But when I think of
educational administration, I fondly think of *If I Ran the Zoo*. With
its complicated layers of systems and controls, the decision-
making ability of a college or school district can be dizzying. It
can seem like running a zoo. Who is in charge of what? When
was that decided? Why wasn't I asked to join this committee? Or
worse: "Why <u>was</u> I asked to join this committee?"

I think the California Community Colleges have a
civilized approach to the tangled strands of institutional decision-
making. There is a systematic model, created under California's
<u>AB 1725</u>, that provides a blueprint for who is involved in what
areas of decision-making. Who has primacy? Whose opinions
are "relied upon?" Who advises the Board and administration on
all matters? If you read <u>AB 1725</u>, you will see that there is

actually a plan to deliver the world's largest system of higher education from the analysis paralysis that can develop when trying to put together stakeholders to make a decision in an *ad hoc* manner. It is by no means a perfect system but it give the colleges a methodology for decision-making.

So who does "run the zoo?" Who really makes the decisions at your educational institution? Before you reach for and consult your Board Policy Manual, consider this: Can you spend your budget on your materials with only your approval? Do you make purchases or "purchase requests?" When you get your paperwork back from the Department of Finance, do you see layers of approvals, initials and stamps on the form? Each one of those layers could be another approval that you actually needed before you could actually purchase your materials.

Before you come down too harshly on the finance staff for this Über-approval function, also consider that these are well-educated, experienced people who have no desire to make your budget management difficult. They are simply responding to years of experience and trying to avoid mistakes that have been made throughout the history of the department. If budgets are consistently miscoded, then there will probably be a layer of account code verification. And all these layers take staff resources and delay orders.

Perhaps more importantly, however, the layers of approval also remove the authority you thought you had over your own budget. When the Board of Trustees approved the budget with a five to zero vote, you thought you had the authority to spend those funds on behalf of your program. And that should be true. But the Finance Department gets stuck in a bind. They hear about system failures from higher administrators, Board Members, auditors, program managers etc. They are admonished from all sides. If any budget manager makes a mistake, the Finance Department will hear about it in some rather public and permanent records, such as the audit report. So it is no wonder that finance staff recoil into a highly protective environment where rules dictate who really runs the zoo.

The Point: The person who really runs the business of the institution is the one who can stop financial transactions from proceeding. Under Skinny Finance that person is the program manager.

The Bermuda Triangle

There must be a place where unfilled purchase requests go to die. I am sure this is the same place one would find the second sock, lost keys and the missing cufflink. Some universal laws will always prevail, you will lose one sock. But the clients of an educational institution's Finance Department do not need to accept lost and delayed purchase requests.

I asked my assistant one day, where my book was. I had ordered it a month before and, frankly, I forgot about it until I needed it. Frances told me she hadn't seen it but would look. She found the purchase request on the desk of the Director of Fiscal Services. Certainly it did not sit there for a month. It couldn't have. So I went to ask Judy about it.

Judy was serious about her Fiscal Services Department but also knew how to have fun. She has a very delightful personality and sense of humor. She was also a long-time employee of the college. She grew and developed her skills as the college grew from a fledgling status in the 1970's to the healthy, growing college it is today.

Lake Tahoe Community College is nestled in the Sierra Nevada Mountains in California. The campus is located in a beautiful forested meadow. The snow, which falls at least five months of the year, adds to the beauty and charm.

The college started literally in a rented broom closet, with a President and a phone. It was that President's task to assemble faculty, staff and students and begin this new college. He did a remarkable job. For a small community (South Lake Tahoe has only 23,000 residents) Lake Tahoe Community College serves 3,000 students, 1,800 full-time equivalent students. Imagine a college in which more than 1 out of every ten residents enrolls! Well, the math is not that simple because there are more than 23,000 residents in the entire service area of the college. But by any measure, this college has a great impact on the community and the students it serves.

Judy grew up with that college. She developed procedures and processes that started small and grew. She was indeed the heart and soul of the Fiscal Services of the college.

And my purchase request was sitting on her desk. So I had to find out why. And I don't mean that I was critical because I didn't have my book. I was more concerned about a process that would let a book sit in the purchasing process for a month with no feedback to the requestor.

I quickly determined that the request had not been sitting on her desk for a month. Knowing Judy, I would have been very surprised if it had. My purchase request had travelled a long and arduous journey through purchasing, finance and budget. There were pre-approvals, approvals of approvals, account code verification and budget verification. Now I know my assistant, Frances. She is the best. I cannot recall her ever making a mistake. I am sure she did but she was so good that I would stack her up against any accountant for accuracy. And I'd bet on Frances to win every time.

There were no mistakes. The account Frances typed was correct and there was budget available to purchase the book. It was just working its way through the process. So this reveals an obvious question: What kind of process takes a month to purchase a book? Maybe it would have been easier to purchase the book on Amazon.com and request reimbursement later.

The problem was not the staff. It was a process that developed over thirty years of a growing college. Over that period of time, as mistakes were discovered in finance, more layers of control were created. This continues because there is very little time to step back and ask "Why are we doing all this?"

I have written that the President of this college is the best I have ever worked with. This Director of Fiscal Services is great too. Our purchasing agent is very good at his job. Couldn't they, with all their knowledge and experience find a way out? The answer has got to be "yes" but Lake Tahoe Community College has a significant limitation in its FCS. There was no logic to prevent a miscoding of purchases. Consequently, the budget managers used paper requisitions to make purchase requests. It was up to the fiscal services staff to verify account codes, budget, "appropriateness" and to enter it into the FCS. This takes time and it develops a Bermuda Triangle effect. The requests go somewhere but nobody can easily and quickly say where.

A Skinny Finance flattens the work process to the point where data is entered by the program budget manager and that data is seamlessly passed to purchasing and accounts payable. Notice the steps that are missing. There is no budget verification; there is no account code entry; there is no verification of "appropriateness." In Skinny Finance these verifications are done at the point of entry by the budget manager.

The Point: A symptom of chubby finance is the disappearance of purchasing documents and delayed delivery of supplies and materials.

Redneck Rampage

"You have got to see this one," the Director of Finance told me. "DSP&S (Disabled Students Programs & Services) ordered Redneck Rampage." Redneck Rampage is a computer game that features gun-toting "gentlemen" who rumble across the countryside in a pickup truck drinking beer and shooting at everything that moves and at those that don't move too. Why on Earth would this Student Services program want a game that is bigoted, drunken and violent? The answer is easy. They don't want it. They simply looked up computer games to aid the students and misread the label. They thought they were ordering "Reading Rampage."

More than the cheap computer game, what I was concerned about was why my Fiscal Services staff was looking so carefully at the content of the purchases rather than refining the system of financial control. I have many highly paid, well-educated and intelligent people in this department and they have lowered their work level to reviewing the "appropriateness" of expenditures. OK, I don't like the fact that taxpayers' dollars went to purchasing this piece of software but I am not willing to sacrifice the heart of financial control so that we can catch the one bizarre expenditure that is made in the district each year. To be completely honest, the determination of "appropriateness" should be vested with the program budget manager, not with the Finance Department staff. Sure I would like to intercept bizarre purchases but at what cost does that review come? Is it worth it?

What is at the heart of this question is also the inner-working of Skinny Finance. We need to move away from transaction-based finance and toward a process-based system. We need to eliminate bottlenecks where well-intending finance staff feels the need to scrutinize each line of each purchase request. So why does the staff do it? For what are they looking?

You can summarize the actions of the Department of Finance into one of three categories or layers:

1. Review to ensure proper account code is used (and that the code exists, for that matter).
2. Review to ensure the purchase has appropriate approval, including budget.
3. Review the purchase for "appropriateness".

The first level of review is fairly simple. The staff is concerned about whether the FCS will even recognize the transaction. Because if an account code does not exist, the default budget value will be zero and the budget would be overdrawn. Even worse, the FCS may reject the transaction with an errant code and then also reject all other transactions batched with it. This can cause a time-consuming fix to the error. It is thought that catching the account code error before the computer system sees the transaction, will save time in the long run. A simpler, skinnier solution would be to have the program budget manager enter the request online. The FCS would only display valid account codes. This will completely eliminate the possibility that a non-existent account code is used. If there is an exception to the validation process, the manager can then call the Department of Finance to resolve the failed validation. In the absence of an FCS that allows online orders by budget managers, the system could, at the very least, use more sophisticated error handlers so that one bad account code does not stop a batch of transactions.

The second layer of review is a set of evaluations that determine whether a purchase has proper authorization. Just as you would think, the Finance Department proceeds logically through their set of routines:

A. Is there budget for the expenditure?
B. Did the manager in charge of the budget approve the expenditure?
C. Did the expenditure require special approval by a committee or a higher manager?

These are all logical and objective tests of a proposed expenditure and it would be hard for any of us to argue against performing these tests. And I am stating that we not only continue to do these but we raise the level of importance to where errors are very rare. When I look at this short list of verifications, I see a set of facts, in the form of the purchase request, and a set of rules, in the form of budgets and policies. Whenever I see that combination of facts compared to rules, I immediately ask, "Why doesn't a computer do this?" A computer is much less likely to make an error and it can audit the purchase requests much faster than can staff members.

But what about the many exceptions to the rules? That is where we need our well-educated, highly-paid Finance

Department staff to spend their time. By avoiding the tedium of transaction-based review and analysis, there is significant time freed to develop systems to handle errors and unusual conditions. Remember the example of the Lamplighter? I had an accountant who was preparing a report of Board expenditures every month, just in case the Director of Finance was asked about boondoggles. She was dealing with an exception in reporting. While it was her bane that she review receipts and pay actions endlessly, she had no power to control the workflow. She was stuck in her position doomed to work at a transaction-based level.

Here is my general law regarding computer logic: Any repetitive task that requires an employee to objectively evaluate a fact against a set of rules, can be completed by a computer, by an FCS.

Where does your Department of Finance find these rules? On a macro level, they are very easy to find. The Board Policies and Administrative Procedures are the official set of rules by which we are asked to operate. The adopted budget is the specific set of rules that apply to a given period of time.

There are sets of rules contained within those documents that provide the vast majority of logic by which the FCS should operate. In Skinny Finance, it is the primary responsibility of the Department of Finance to develop those rules into the logic sets that the FCS uses. This will stop the tedious transaction-based review process that has probably developed over the history of the institution. This is a chief goal of Skinny Finance to eliminate repetition of transaction-based review by the Department of Finance.

The third layer of review that a Department of Finance often performs is the subjective test of the "appropriateness" of expenditures. This is a subjective review that is not easily performed by the FCS. How does a computer know if Redneck Rampage is appropriate for the disabled students program? It does not. But, you might also ask, how can the Finance Department know if it is appropriate? I assert it does not know what is appropriate. Sure the staff can provide a special level of scrutiny for purchases that seem out of the ordinary but, under Skinny Finance, the transaction-based review is replaced by a more robust system review. By eliminating the transaction-based review, the test of "appropriateness" must be transferred out of

the Department of Finance. The Department would more

logically leave the review of appropriateness of expenditures to

the budget manager who originated the request.

The Redneck Rampage example is an odd occurrence

and we should not base systems solely to catch this error at the

level where it was found. It should be found at the program level.

What would be the consequences if the Department of Finance

makes a mistake in their subjective review of "appropriateness?"

I have an acquaintance who was studying the effects of aging.

He had placed an order for a certain chemical, provided by a

certain vendor on a specified timeline. The Purchasing

Department received the request. In its review, the staff

determined that another vendor could deliver the same chemical

for a lesser cost. So what is the harm? Process the order with

the new vendor. Unfortunately, this chemical breaks down

quickly and time is of the essence when performing this certain

experiment. The chemical arrived late and was degraded but my

scientist friend did not know. So he proceeded with the

experiment only to find that all of his previous findings were rejected by the current experiment. He later discovered the problem was with the chemical that was actually delivered versus what he had ordered.

In this case, it is easy to see that the budget manager, the researcher, knew far more about the "appropriateness" of the expenditure and the well-intending Department of Finance substituted their judgment for his. It was a complete system failure. The cost of the chemical was wasted, the research time was wasted and the researcher was discouraged by not only the lack of accurate results but also by the fact that an accountant second-guessed the "appropriateness" of his purchase.

In this example, what value was added by the Department of Finance performing that third layer of review?

From an organizational development perspective, this failed purchase did more harm than to just the experiment. It sent a signal to the campus community that the Department of Finance knows more about your instructional or research program than you do. I have worked with some excellent instructional administrators and faculty over the years. And I have worked with some who did not excel. But every one of them knew their subject material better than I did. What? I have

a BA in Economics, MBA in Finance, certificate of School

Business Management and an Ed.D. in Organizational

Leadership, I have decades of experience working in schools,

colleges and universities, yet someone knows more than me.

Does that mean I am a failure in my chosen field of educational

business management? Not at all. It is reality. I will never know

more about Theatre Arts than David Hamilton at Lake Tahoe

Community College. I will never know as much about Computer

and Information Science as does Jill Malone, the department

chair at MiraCosta College. Their professions are to deliver

excellent instruction in their departments and I cannot compete

in that regard.

Often nobody wants to resist the Department of Finance

because they cannot compete in the world of financial rules and

administrative procedures. This is a world in which I have

excelled in my career. But I need to recognize that I cannot, nor

should I try, to compete to know more about instructional

delivery than the administrators and faculty in those areas. So,

while some budget managers quietly dissent from the test of

"appropriateness" they rarely speak so directly about it that a

Finance Department understands the concern. If finance did

understand then they would want to move away from this

transactional analysis.

To this point I have focused on the consequences of a

failed test of "appropriateness." There is another significant

concern that deserves consideration. Budget managers have

feelings like all other humans and it does not feel good to be

second-guessed, especially in your own area of expertise.

When I was a young twenty-something year old

administrator, I saw a reimbursement request for a group of

faculty who went to San Francisco for a conference. I saw one of

the receipts read: "Massage $250." I tested the

"appropriateness" of the expenditure. My first impression was

that the college should not pay $250 for a faculty member's

personal massage. Rather than make a big production out of it, I

went to the faculty member and asked him about the expense. I

told him that it would not look good if the auditor randomly

selected this transaction and I had paid for the faculty to be

pampered. Fortunately, this faculty member was a friend and

had some compassion for me and my youthful exuberance. He calmly told me, "The conference was to learn how to teach massage. That is the class I teach." Oops. I was convinced that I had stumbled upon a receipt representing scandalous affairs. I was concerned how it would look in the newspapers. But I didn't stop to think that this was a fully authorized expenditure for a service that was part of the curriculum.

So what do we do about the real scandalous affairs that will eventually occur? Under Skinny Finance, we train budget managers and make clear that their authorization is the "last line of defense" for "appropriateness." We educate the campus to understand and embrace a new culture where budget managers carefully review their own expenditures and do not rely upon the Department of Finance to use this subjective, transaction-based review to test for "appropriateness."

And we have a road map to help the budget managers. By tying all expenditures to a Strategic Goal of the institution, the budget managers are bound by those goals. When expenditures are made, they must attach to a specific goal. If it does not, the expense is not in pursuit of a goal and must be eliminated or a new goal must be adopted by the campus community to

accommodate the expenditure.

The Point: Skinny Finance relies upon computers to

perform the repeated comparison of facts to rules and it asks

budget managers to review their own purchases for

"appropriateness" in the context of the Strategic Goals of the

institution.

Part Three – Assessing Readiness for Skinny Finance

Culture of the Institution

Is your Finance Department often feared by other

departments on campus? Is there a general feeling that nobody

knows what goes on behind the thick doors of Accounting?

When other departments speak of the Finance Department, is it

praise or criticism? You would, of course, recognize these

questions as a way to assess your need for Skinny Finance but

not all institutions of education are ready for the leaner, more

customer service oriented administration. The first step in

developing a Skinny Finance is to assess the culture of the

institution.

Investigation of the culture of readiness can begin with the Finance Department and this is a logical place to start. But it is not your only option. Having a Finance Department that is ready, certainly makes the transformation to a Skinny Finance easier. And if the Finance staff supports the move and leads the transition, Skinny Finance will result from simply focusing on the new culture. But to assess readiness for a Skinny Finance, you may want to ask the budget managers first. Do they want the change?

Ask open-ended questions of the managers. How would you describe the business processes of the institution? From your perspective, how well do you think it functions? If you have a chubby finance system, then you will hear about slow deliveries and paperwork that disappears for long periods of time. Comments may hover around the issue of desiring a leaner finance but the managers may not actually state it aloud. Why?

Perhaps the biggest reason that people shy away from providing honest feedback to the Finance Department is that the department seems unapproachable. They have so many rules that most of the campus community could not begin to compete against the Finance Department's knowledge of business services. Another reason for less-than-candid review of the Finance Department is that the budget managers need their expenditures to flow smoothly. In my career, I have never seen a Department of Finance intentionally slow someone's expenditure. But the threat may be out there as a misunderstanding. This misperception is aggravated when the Finance Department does ensure that the Superintendents and Presidents get their requests filled faster than other budget managers. If the Department of Finance will expedite one person's request, might they slow a request from someone providing candid feedback?

With an honest cultural appraisal of the entire institution, you can then go to the Department of Finance and take a look at their culture. Are they heavily steeped in tradition, rules and procedures? Do they adopt new ideas quickly? Have they tried new procedures and succeeded? And failed? How did they respond to the failures? All of these answers indicate the readiness of the culture of the Department of Finance to adopt a

Skinny Finance. But please do not be misled. It takes quite a bit of work to conduct these cultural assessments. I would recommend that before you begin this process, you hire a professional who knows psychology, group dynamics and finance.

So what exactly are you, or your professional consultant looking for? I will follow with a list of the exact right culture that would be clearly ready to adopt Skinny Finance. It is helpful to compare your actual culture with this list but it is not the complete measurement of cultural readiness.

The Director of Finance has formal education and has been exposed to other ideas.	The Department of Finance is a flat organization with dynamic lines of communication.	The Department of Finance has tried a new procedure and succeeded.	The Department of Finance has tried a new procedure and failed but was supported and encouraged by the cabinet and Board.
The Department of Finance knows they create delays in purchases or personnel requisitions.	The Department of Finance cares about how they work with other departments.	The Department of Finance has a history of asking for new tools.	The Finance staff talks about the process more than the transactions.
The Department of Finance staff frequently volunteers for projects and committees outside of Finance.	The Department of Finance staff has deep personal relationships with the staff of the Information Technology Department.	The Department of Finance is active in the audit process. They do not wait for results. They direct the auditor to areas that need attention.	The Department of Finance communicates with the campus community regularly.
Other campus constituencies are invited to participate in finance work groups.	The chief business official has a history of supporting the Department of Finance.	The Governing Board knows what the Department of Finance does.	The Chief Executive of the institution receives updates from the Department of Finance.
The Department of Finance provides training for budget managers on a regular basis.	At least one person in the Department of Finance has formal or experiential knowledge of computer programming.	In an audit, the Director of Finance is the advocate of the departments, not an advocate of the auditor.	At least one person in the Department of Finance has formal education in Organizational Development.

Signs of Ideal Culture for Change to Skinny Finance

This matrix provides signals of the ideal cultural

conditions under which Skinny Finance can be successfully

implemented. I recommend you take this matrix to your cabinet and walk through each box. If you feel one applies to your current Department of Finance, leave it blank. If it does not apply, draw an "X" across the box. If you have more "X"'s than blank squares, you may want to consider hiring an Organization Development consultant <u>who knows finance</u>. If you have predominantly blank squares, your staff is probably already trying to reach a level of Skinny Finance. Maybe they need support or a slight nudge to achieve the more customer-oriented Skinny Finance culture.

The Point: The culture of the institution must be right to implement a Skinny Finance.

Financial Control Systems

My father and I built a computer when I was a young teenager. We sat together soldering transistors, resistors and capacitors to a board, linked cables to other boards and eventually had a fully working model. My father had a B.S. in Electrical Engineering and Computer Sciences from Iowa State University and a J.D. from the University of San Diego. We put the new computer through a bunch of tests and finally it performed exactly how it was intended.

My first assignment: print my name to the screen. Easy. Now print it to the screen 1,000 times. The computer didn't complain; it just did it. I asked my dad, "What can I actually do with the computer?" I wanted something of value. He explained that eventually computers would replace all the redundant tasks that we perform. He challenged me to perform my next homework assignment on the computer and turn it in. The next day, my typing instructor asked all of us to type a page full of that all-too-classic pangram: "The quick brown fox jumps over the lazy dog." And she wanted a whole page of that? I would give her reams of paper full of the sentence if she wanted. I knew how to program the computer.

After my assignment was turned in to the instructor, I heard a few questions about why the paper was so wide and why it had white and green bars. But my assignment was technically completed. I received a passing grade in the class. But to this day, I still hunt and peck for the keys. I should have done the assignment properly.

To me my father was a superhero but he did not invent the microcomputer. He did, however, create in me a model that was indelibly printed in my mind. Endless tasks, repetition, Mathematics, rules and logic could all be programmed into that little box that hummed away at my feet. Anything I was asked to do that required the same task over and over could be asked of the computer. I loved it. My next programming quest was to write a program that could play me in a game of chess. Thirty years later, I am not quite done with that one.

Skip ahead with me to the 21st century. I am watching how my finance staff interacts with the computer. I am working with them to understand that the computer alone does nothing. There is a system of human input that provides data to the FCS. Humans also develop the logic of the FCS, which then evaluates the data against a series of rules established by programmers responding to the needs of finance. So the computer, taken alone, is worthless to a Department of Finance. There must be an interaction that includes: a set of rules, the Finance Department, input from other budget managers and the FCS. Unfortunately, at every educational institution where I have worked, one of those pieces was missing.

By law, public educational institutions must have budgets, policies and procedures. So the rules were all there. In each of my professional positions, there has also been a finance staff that interacts with the FCS. The piece typically missing is the interaction among the budget managers and the FCS. Since others are not using the computer system regularly, the rules and logic established for the FCS focus on the needs of the current users of the FCS, the finance staff.

By overlaying what my father taught me about repetitive

tasks, I can see that writing checks, entering invoices and

establishing fixed asset inventories are all functions that the

finance staff completes routinely through the FCS.

Unfortunately, some of the more tedious tasks are performed by

hand. Review of account codes, review for authorization and

review for appropriateness have been completed by hand at

each institution where I have worked. Well at least they were all

performed by hand when I arrived.

Let's break down those repetitive tasks:

1. Review to ensure proper account code is used
2. Review to ensure the purchase has appropriate
   approval
3. Review the purchase for "appropriateness"

The first and second tasks are functions of comparing

data (purchase requisitions, personnel actions etc.) to a set of

rules, the budget, policies and procedures. I argue that the third

layer of validation should be removed from the Department of

Finance and placed in the hands of the budget managers who

know infinitely more about the program needs than finance could

ever know.

So if the first and second tasks are repetitive, can we not get the computer to perform these? Certainly. The FCS and, frankly, the Information Technology staff are waiting to be asked. What would that look like to automate verification of account codes and authorization?

Any halfway decent FCS can provide online requisitions to budget managers. Why have you not seen it? The reason is usually that the Department of Finance has decommissioned that functionality so that finance can continue the detailed review of each transaction. As stated earlier, this level of review does add value but it comes at a huge cost in staff time and in the integrity of the system. Under Skinny Finance, we need to let loose that function and allow the budget managers to enter the purchase data once, and only once. The FCS is fully capable of validating account codes and checking for budget and approvals.

The point in this evaluation is to assess your FCS as a complete system, including the human input from budget managers and finance staff. Are the users ready to integrate their activities with a decentralized FCS? If the question is properly framed with the staff, the answer must be "yes." There would be no legitimate reason that a person already preparing the requisition to not want to do it in the error-free environment of the FCS. The key is in properly framing the questions so that the end users arrive at the conclusion using their own logic.

So what happens if your FCS cannot perform these user-end validation functions? Immediately ask your vendor why you do not have this functionality. If the module has been decommissioned, then commission it and begin exploring the new integrated management system. If the vendor adamantly states that the control of budget entries cannot be decentralized, start looking for a new vendor. I have no patience for a system that cannot perform 1990's technology in the 21st century. Even worse, if you consider that the FCS vendor cannot provide this simple functionality, imagine all the other, more cutting-edge, technologies that you are missing from your system.

The Point: Your software (FCS) is probably ready to execute decentralized Skinny Finance. The challenge is to evaluate readiness in terms of the integrated human / software / hardware system.

The Navigation System

I don't know about you but I am hooked on my car's new navigation system. How simple can driving possibly get? Simply type in an address and the car will determine where you are, where you need to go and how to get there. Similarly Skinny Finance is simple in that regard. If you have a well-designed navigation system, you will know where you are, where you are heading and how to get there. But like a car's system, if you do not program a destination, you will not go anywhere.

"Wherever you go, there you are." Buckaroo Banzai.

So where does this Skinny Finance find its destination to use in the new navigation system? The best place to begin is the Strategic Goals and Objectives of the educational institution. The previous manual drafting course example is a clear case where the Academic Senate, Instructional Administration and a Skinny Finance Department can re-allocate funds based upon what best serves the mission of the educational institution and achieves its Strategic Goals. This is the destination in the navigation system of the institution: Strategic Goals.

"But my district does not have an automatic navigation system," you might say. When you adopt the Skinny Finance program, it does. You just need to learn how it navigates. Skinny Finance relies heavily upon goals and objectives so that is the first place to start. You will find time for this by eliminating the redundancies of transaction-based workflow. In this context, all you need to know is that your navigation system starts with the Mission, Strategic Goals and Objectives.

We all have elaborate charts of accounts. By looking at one 24-digit code from MiraCosta College, I could tell you what the expenditure was, where it was spent, how it was funded and in what fiscal year it was incurred. I could even tell you who authorized the expenditure. You know what I could not tell you? I could not tell you why we spent the money. That is pretty sad. We committed millions of dollars to staff and computer resources to control the financial resources of the college but I could not look at an account and tell you why we spent the money in the first place. For Skinny Finance, that will simply not do. We need to know why money is spent.

With the power of a modern FCS a Finance Department can add account codes until reports are endless streams of numbers, and sometimes they do. But I propose we add a simple two-digit field to the account code structure. In a perfectly skinny world of finance, what would I put in that field? I would put "why" we spent the money. In pursuit of what Strategic Goal did we make this expenditure?

In my first attempt to implement this system, I was told by the finance staff, "most of the expenditures do not fall under a Strategic Goal or objective." My answer was simple. "Don't expend the funds if they do not move the college closer to our Strategic Goals." That is pretty simple but there was significant resistance. What about raises for the faculty? In a typical year, there is some increase in step and column and a net raise across the board. This is not a Strategic Goal. Oh, yes it is, under Skinny Finance.

Look back at your Strategic Plan. Does it not say something like: "It is the goal of this educational Institution to recruit, train and retain the best faculty to benefit our students?"

Then could we not say that a pay raise to all faculty helps to

recruit and retain the faculty? I think that if a faculty member

were hired right out of graduate school and didn't receive any

increase in compensation, that faculty member would likely

leave, pretty quickly. So salaries of faculty are goal-oriented.

The salaries recruit and retain the best faculty we can afford for

our students.

Like our car's navigation systems, we will not reach the

destination (Strategic Goals) of the institution if we do not

program the destination into the institution's navigation system.

We need to look at each expenditure from the point of view that

it must have an associated Strategic Goal. At this point, you may

say that this creates a chubby finance, mired in the details of

transactional analysis. But by working on the front end to load

your FCS with a chart of accounts that assigns goals to each

line of appropriation, then the finance staff can eliminate the

need to review each transaction. As explained elsewhere in this

book, avoiding this transactional analysis is at the heart of how

to develop a Skinny Finance Department. We will work

rigorously on the front end to make sure our navigation system is programmed to reach Strategic Goals and then we will leave the assignment of individual expenditures to the program administrators.

The Point: Skinny Finance requires a clear Strategic Plan to use as a destination setting in the institution's navigation system.

Part Four – Implementation

Homeless in San Diego

When I was an undergraduate at the University of California at San Diego, then Mayor of "The Finest City in America," Maureen O'Connor was elected after Rodger Hedgecock resigned. While she was Mayor, O'Connor spent some time living on the streets with the homeless. She had a need to fully understand the plight and culture of the homeless people in the city. Living undercover she met and interacted with the homeless and absorbed their culture. When she resurfaced in her Mayoral persona, O'Connor was dedicated to help her less fortunate neighbors she had met and to carry their culture and message to others who could help them.

It is reported that she began her next City Council meeting with many homeless in the audience. She was connecting the dots. These people have no jobs and they want to work. The City of San Diego has hundreds of vacant jobs in the Department of General Services. Filling potholes and raking leaves is not glamorous work, but if I were unemployed and homeless, I would welcome the opportunity to do this work. She challenged the city managers. Find these people work. Then she addressed the homeless in the chamber, "leave your phone numbers with the clerk and I promise someone will contact you," she was reported to have said.

How could we not applaud her effort to connect with the culture and values of the homeless? It is an urban problem that needs a civic solution. While I often disagreed with Mayor O'Connor's politics, her attempt to learn the culture of the people on the streets was well-received. Unfortunately, with one well-intended but insensitive comment, she unraveled her plan. She understood what it was like to sleep under a bridge but forgot that San Diego's homeless, in the 1980's did not have phones. How could they leave phone numbers with the city managers?

What application does this have to the implementation of Skinny Finance? I am certainly not comparing the culture of the Department of Finance to that of homeless people but if we are not careful to fully understand the culture of the Department of Finance, we could easily commit a faux pas on a project-ending scale.

The Point: Fully understand the culture of the people you intend to help before you attempt to help them.

L. Edwin Coate

A student at MiraCosta College had been issued a financial aid check. She reported it lost or stolen. So my Finance Department followed procedure. They canceled the check and reissued the student another check. Unbeknownst to the college, as soon as we reissued the check, someone with identification matching that of the student, cashed the original check. Then the student cashed the new check. The canceled check notice came to our department. Shortly thereafter, a notice of legal action arrived on my desk. The check cashing store that received the canceled check wanted their money. I called and explained to the store that the student had lost the check. So we stopped the payment and reissued. I further explained that the store would need to contact the person who cashed the check for repayment.

This news was not well-received by the store. The woman with whom I spoke also said that she would sue the college for the money but that it was nothing out of the ordinary for her. Check cashing stores are in a habit of suing issuers of checks who stop payments. Sure enough, a notice of the lawsuit arrived on my desk soon thereafter. The college was being sued for $1,172 the amount of the stopped check. I immediately brought this to the attention of my boss, Dr. L. Edwin (Ed) Coate, the Vice President of Business Services for the college.

Ed asked me what I wanted to do. He asked me how I felt about it. What difference does it matter how I feel about it? We needed to fix the situation that is how I feel about it.

"No," Ed continued, "how do you feel about your staff following procedure and ending up in a small claims suit?" So I told him. I let him have it. Turning my emotions on Ed, one person who did not deserve it, I told him, "I am pissed off. That student could be defrauding us and has used the store to perpetrate this fraud scheme." Ed had a cute, knowing smile. "You are right to be pissed. I am pissed about that too. And I am pissed because they made you pissed. What do you want to do about it?"

Ed was smart. He was doing something I would not learn about for another twelve years – not until I was in my doctoral program. He was pacing me and my emotions. He was helping me through the emotions that we all feel in finance. But the culture of finance is such that we cannot show emotion. Everything is business. We have rules for everything and we follow the rules. Unfortunately, in this situation, there was no rule. And Dr. L. Edwin Coate had a twenty-something year old Director who was confused about the disruption to his plan and was pissed off about the potential crime committed against his college. It was a direct assault against me, personally! It was not a victimless crime. It was not washed away in the sea of tax dollars we receive every year. I was angry that someone was impeaching the integrity of my Finance Department.

"So what do you want to do about it?" Ed asked again.

I defiantly answered, "These check cashing stores are probably so used to filing undefended lawsuits that it is no big deal to them." Well it was a big deal to me; my department's integrity was under attack. "Let's defend the lawsuit," I answered. Ed smiled again. "Sure. You defend the lawsuit. Prepare for it and go to court on behalf of the college." He reminded me that I could not use an attorney in small claims

court.

I consulted with my father who was a lawyer and I

studied the law on my own. My father's first advice was to pay

the bill and move forward. "How much is your time worth to the

college that you can take this time to defend a small claim?" my

father asked. But, like Ed, my father was also interested in

developing my character. So he too encouraged me to prepare

for and defend the lawsuit. And I was onto a solid defense. To

issue funds from a federal student aid program twice for the

same claim violates the <u>FEDERAL</u> laws concerning financial aid

programs. Oh, that is brilliant. I am going to win this suit. Any

suit where you have federal law on your side must be winnable.

I got my clocked cleaned. I lost the suit in about thirty

seconds of actual trial time.

I reported back to Ed. He was compassionate and

understanding, in a mentoring / fatherly way. "Don't worry about

it. You have a big budget to manage and lots to do outside of the

courtroom." But he had to ask, "Are you still pissed off?"

Strangely, I wasn't. I was embarrassed that I lost but I wasn't pissed off any more. I learned later in life that this is an effective way to develop a young administrator. Pace the emotions. Get to a level where it is clear what the feelings are and then work backwards to a logical position that solves the problem. Don't let the emotions drive the administrator to a point where he responds from the emotions.

So Ed and I headed off to the college President's office. Lawsuits of any size need to be reported to the President, the rest of cabinet and the Board. Yikes, the Board would know. How humiliating for me.

We sat in front of Dr. Dong, another excellent administrator with whom I have had the privilege of working. "What happened?" asked Dr. Dong. I started to speak but Ed cut me off. "Well, Tim," Ed began. I would never have called the President by his first name, Tim. Maybe that is a privilege one gets when one becomes Vice President but I was *just* a Director. "Tim," Ed said. "I saw an opportunity to test the security of fraudulently cashing a financial aid check and for a check cashing store to honor a canceled check. I thought that by defending the small claim suit, we could head off the future

students who may see check cashing stores as a source of...."
What the hell? My name didn't come up once. What was Ed
doing? Was he taking the blame? No, there was no blame. Ed
was accounting for the actions of his departments in the first
person.

At that moment, I vowed that I would always support my
staff in this same way.

How would this apply to the implementation of Skinny
Finance? I hope there are many lessons in this short story but
the biggest is this: Let your Finance Department try and fail. And
when they do fail, pick up the pieces <u>with</u> them, not <u>for</u> them.
Understand that the Finance Department lives in a complex set
of rules that are handed down from multiple sources. The staff is
risk-adverse. When they do take a risk, support it because it is a
rare event.

This also implies that you may need to nudge the
administrator in charge of the department to take that risk. Your
promise to support them if they fail means something but the
administrator needs to see the support on small risks. Then they

will, hopefully, develop a culture where risk-taking in regard to a new FCS and culture is possible.

The Point: Support your Finance Director, especially in failures. When a person is emotionally broken and discouraged, that is a very teachable moment.

City Softball

What work of great literature would be complete without a sports analogy?

I played in a city softball league after work on Tuesday nights. Our team had no mascot but we were sponsored by Tri-Electric Supply. We had nice uniforms and a pretty good team. We won far more games than we lost. I would like to tell you that I was the star of the team but that simply was not true. I was not in the top three on the team nor was I in the bottom three for softball talent. I was average. While loving the game and my team, I hated mediocrity. In all areas of my life, I have wanted to excel. And who doesn't?

I was disappointed when Bobby Demaray was chosen to play shortstop. I was relegated to second base. Honestly, Bobby was a better player and better athlete than I was but that didn't make me feel better about my "demotion" to second base.

In one season, like the prior season, we easily made the playoffs. I think just about all the teams make the playoffs, much

99

like the NBA. We were playing a game and in the final inning we had a three run lead. All we needed were three easy outs and we would be done. The first batter was out. The second got a base hit. Error, error and we were down to a two run lead. We had another error and we had a one run lead before a batter hit a line drive out to third base. We were one out away from winning. We were waiting for the final pitch and the final out. But the repeated errors echoed in our minds. The batter popped the ball straight up in the air just behind the pitcher. Our pitcher moved toward it, Bobby from shortstop moved toward it, I moved toward it. None of us wanted to drop the third out and nobody was calling for the ball. Finally I yelled loudly, "I've got it." Immediately the other two players moved back.

I called loudly not just to get those two away from me but I did it for myself. I absolutely positively would catch the ball. I don't know why earlier in the inning, players better than me made the errors but I knew I would not make an error. It was a simple pop fly. The game should be won in just a second. And as we all hoped, the ball gently landed in my glove; the game was over. Boy did I get a lot of congratulations. Bobby, the much better player, told me as we walked off, "When you called it, I knew you were going to catch the ball." Why was everyone so relieved that I caught the ball? Well, I will tell you what I didn't say that evening. I was relieved too. I played it off like there was no pressure but there was significant pressure on me to catch a simple pop fly.

I said our team was good. We stopped grounders, caught flies, fielded short-hops and every other kind of ball someone could hit. We usually stopped everything hit at us. But on this evening, in the final inning, we were not playing to win the game. We were each playing to <u>not lose</u>. Oh, Stephens is playing a game of semantics here. Winning and not losing are the same, right? No. They are very different.

When you approach your Department of Finance about adopting Skinny Finance, you need to understand the predominant culture in finance. Finance often plays to <u>not lose</u>. A Finance Department does not necessarily play to win. But it is equally important to understand that there is usually someone in the Finance Department who is discontent with <u>not losing</u>. They want to win. They are willing to take chances with the understanding that they may not emerge victorious with trumpets playing. So who is that key player in the Finance Department? Who will catch the third out to win the game rather than to not lose?

With all sincerity I hope this winner is your Director of Finance. I have tried to play the finance game by taking chances and trying to win. And I have lost a few: reference the small claims court case. But it was in that loss that I learned, with L. Edwin Coate's help, that I could take other chances and win. Remember that your Director of Finance was promoted to this position because of intelligence, a great education, excellent experience and the person has navigated a career without losing. That does not mean the Director won all of the battles but the battles were not lost either.

Just like I did in the softball game, your Director of Finance will likely get under the ball and say, "I must catch this ball because I do not want to lose the game." The Director who is ready for Skinny Finance will station herself under the ball and declare, "I am going to catch this ball to win the game."

So what happens if the Director is not the risk-taker you

need to implement Skinny Finance? First you need to find out

the personalities of your players. If I were your administrator,

you would learn quickly that I am willing to take risks that have a

high potential to benefit the campus community. If students,

faculty, staff, administration or the Board stand to benefit from a

new initiative, then I am the person to implement the idea. And if

I lose, I will learn something and move on to the next best idea.

But this has come after decades of experience and having

complete support from excellent mentors and bosses. Guy

Lease, referenced earlier, is a great supporter of risk-taking. He

encourages the administration of his college to aggressively

think beyond current limitations. His planning sessions are full of

the phrase "OK, but if we did have the money and time, what

could we do?" You need to assume that your Department of

Finance may not have the positive supportive experiences that I

have had. Maybe they did lose a battle and really felt the loss.

That is part of the culture of the Department of Finance. With

proper support, the loss can be positive. Without support, the

department may stop generating new ideas.

So you practice with your Department of Finance, just like a coach leads practice in softball. You lob balls up and see who routinely catches them. You declare, "If this next ball is dropped, you will all run laps around the field." Who steps under *that* ball to catch it? It matters much less that the person actually catches the ball. You want to see who steps up for the challenge.

Applying that to a campus environment, gives a challenging and new idea that requires a little risk-taking. Watch how the Finance Department responds. I'll bet that if you properly phrase the project as a non-mission critical pilot that will be evaluated and not necessarily implemented, someone other than the Director of Finance will step forward.

The Point: Understand that the Finance Department has been rewarded for not taking risks. This is part of their culture.

The Zebra

One of the recent challenges for educational finance has been the inventory of fixed assets. In my college, at the time, it was no different. The Governmental Accounting Standards Board (GASB) was requiring that the items purchased for public schools and colleges be inventoried. This was the early 1990's when we started to review the proposed requirement and, believe it or not, public schools and colleges had no inventory systems. I saw this as a golden opportunity to merge some FCS systems that did not communicate with each other. We could take purchase requests, issue purchase orders, receive the items and generate an inventory with one level of data entry, the purchase request. That data would pass seamlessly from system to system, eliminating possible sources of error and redundant work.

Technologically, this was a piece of cake. Administratively, however, this would take some wrangling.

Purchasing and Receiving didn't report to me. Similar to the Finance Department, these departments had a culture of conservatism. They didn't want to take risks. But my idea would not gain traction without the integration of their work and data systems.

Thinking back to how L. Edwin Coate encouraged me to try new things, I thought I would see how my staff would respond to a challenge. I was intending to lob a ball and see who wanted to win the game enough to get under it. I developed the key components:

1. The challenge had no simple solution.
2. It was meaningful. Auditors would eventually check our work.
3. There was no promise that the solution would be the final system. It was a prototype.
4. It would involve risk. With no rules to govern the new inventory system, someone would have to develop something new.
5. It had a real life application.
6. It involved people outside of the Department of Finance.

An accountant from the college bookstore stepped forward. As we talked about this new project, the accountant from the bookstore started to camp under the ball. "I think my enterprise accounting system in the bookstore has an inventory system that links to the general ledger," she said. "I know it is not district wide but it could be a place to start." I asked her to look into it and make a proposal of cost, time and commitments from other departments she would need to implement a plan.

It took her, maybe, a week to prepare a proposal. The cost was under $500. She would need help from Purchasing, Receiving and Computer Services. As far as I could tell, she was right on target. She explained how we could use this Zebra technology to bar code each item as we received it. The inventory data would come from the purchasing system. We could gather the vendor, model, style, color, everything from the purchasing documents. We would assign black and white striped barcodes to each item. Computer Services could write a little code that would allow us to scan the barcodes to take the inventory.

I will stop there but this accountant from the bookstore had a plan for the inventory prototype developed in a week. It took about a month to implement. Then we had a trial run. We had hoped that we could capture the data where the items should be located for easy inventory. It didn't work. Items in the bookstore were moved, missing, and sold. That part of the system simply failed us. But quickly, Computer Services came up with an exceptions list. "Why don't we record the inventory that we can and then search for exceptions?" asked Phil, an excellent programmer and a heck of a nice guy. Before I knew it, half of the Computer Services Department was in my office drawing new dataflow diagrams on my whiteboard. Accounting staff were there too. "Why don't you integrate the POS system so items sold are automatically removed from inventory?" said a college accountant. "That will take care of 75% of the exceptions."

Obviously the story continues. But what I saw that was truly remarkable is the person who stepped forward to develop this prototype system was not the person I would have expected. She was not the supervisor or the Director. She was a bookstore accountant with a desire to win. Once she had created this atmosphere where chances are taken and no idea is worthless, plenty of people wanted to be on her team.

The Point: Look for leadership in all people, even the people you are sure cannot lead. You may be surprised.

Epilogue to the Zebra:

One cautionary note, however. After completing the prototype system, I was promoted to a higher level administration at another institution. I would be in charge of not only finance but also a large technology division. The bookstore accountant also left to work closer to her home. At that point, the Zebra program died. Nobody stepped under that falling pop fly ball. It was too bad because there was a lot of energy and trust in that team and the program had merit.

Hitting an Invisible Target

What is harder than hitting a moving target? How about hitting a target that doesn't exist yet?

While working as a financial administrator at a California Community College, I received a call from my brother. Kenneth R. Stephens II, or "Rod" to me, is the smartest man I have ever known. He is hands-down brilliant at solving all kinds of technological challenges. He lives to hear the phrase, "we can't do <u>that</u>," because he knows, most of the time you can do <u>that</u>. And he will know how to do <u>that</u>. Whenever I have a technology-based question and I have no clue how to proceed, I call him.

Well on this one day in the very early 1990's, he called me. He wanted to know what email address he could use to communicate with me. Email what? Apparently, he perceived that a new technology was emerging as the dominant way future communications would be handled. Sure, he had email for a while, after all he was a graduate student at M.I.T. But I guess this day he felt like email would soon be available to civilians like his younger brother.

After a bunch of gyrations with a local four-year university, I got my first email account using an email interface called Pine. Shortly thereafter, other college staff found ways to get email using Eudora. Even more email clients emerged on campus. Soon much of the college wanted email and our college had no one platform on which to deliver the service.

So Computer Services retreated to a quiet place and contemplated the range of solutions. Eventually, a working group of other departments joined Computer Services and they developed a plan to implement GroupWise, a Novell product. This work group identified one major problem facing an effective implementation. GroupWise was still under development, it was not installed anywhere on campus, nobody knew how to use it and about 500 employees would simultaneously migrate to it as the standard email client. Aside from those issues, the implementation looked great!

The question remained. How do we hit a target that is not only moving but is also just an idea? We developed an elaborate plan. Computer Services would meet with Novell and learn about what the system would be when implemented. They translated that technical language into the functionality that our users would understand. Computer Services then trained trainers using screen captured images of how the system will look.

Over a weekend, the Computer Services staff finished the installation of the network end and additional staff went to every workstation at the college and installed GroupWise. We asked that nobody turn on their computers when they came to work that morning. We had shut down all of the computer laboratories on campus and had GroupWise installed, ready to train. In a few short hours, we transported the entire staff and faculty of the college to the email age.

Implementing Skinny Finance is very similar. Your institution, hopefully with leadership from your Department of Finance, will chart a course to a destination that is not yet fully defined. You know what the system will do but not how it will do it:

1. It will be customer service oriented.

2. It will expedite and reliably deliver the personnel, materials and supplies ordered.
3. It will be system-based rather than transaction-based.
4. It will build logic into the FCS to avoid the need for redundancy of data entry and avoid transaction review.
5. It will eliminate the Department of Finance's review for "appropriateness" and let budget managers manage their own budgets.
6. It will be soft on the people but rigorous on the system procedures.
7. It will change the way every budget manager conducts business.

To summarize, you need the human process, technology and training to all intersect at some point in the future. Recalling your algebra from junior high, you will remember that a system of equations with four variables (human process, technology, training and time) must be solved simultaneously using four equations. I can determine any one of the variables if you tell me the other three. But in most cases of Skinny Finance implementation, you have four variables and few equations (relationships among the variables). You can pick the time, understanding that this schedule will determine how developed your human process, technology and training can proceed in that amount of time.

From this point, a good organizational leadership consultant can pick from a number of methodologies to simultaneously solve the sequencing of the four variables. Personally I prefer to target an achievable goal that is aggressive enough to get people interested but not so ambitious that staff will be frightened away from the implementation. Then, as we achieve that goal, our team can declare victory and start to adopt future goals. In essence, this staged methodology provides a sequence of successful mini-projects that accumulate into the overall Skinny Finance goal.

The Point: To successfully implement Skinny Finance, an institution needs to plan on hitting a point in time where the human process, technology and training all intersect.

Part Five – Special Notes

Generations

I will just say it. At the time of this writing, I am 44 years old. I have twenty years experience working in schools, colleges and universities. I began my career in education at a young age so I have spent most of my professional life working with people considerably older than I am. Along the way, I have noticed some stark contrasts between "my generation" and that of other administrators. Born in 1963, I may have technically missed the official cut-off for Generation X. I guess nobody told my parents to wait two years so that I could be officially born in the X generation. But I certainly identify with the values and expectations of that group.

"Each generation has distinct attitudes, behaviors, expectations, habits and motivational buttons." (Hammill, 2005)

The following list is intended to give you a glimpse into the characteristics of Generation X. The reason that these views are important is that many of your new employees in the Finance Department will share these values. As members of my generation become the senior administrators, you will see a cultural shift that is independent from the culture of finance in general and it is different from the educational institution's culture. Some of these new personality traits will innocuously integrate into existing culture: working in teams, for instance. Some of the personality traits, however, may cause disruption to the conservative culture of the Finance Department. For instance, demanding an automated solution after performing a repetitious task will sound revolutionary to a more senior generation. To the Generation X, an automated solution for all things repetitious is our birthright.

There will be tension in the finance culture to remain conservative and use traditional transactional analysis in the face of the newly entering Generation X-ers. Previous generations will be diametrically opposed to the Generation X

employees who want it all done without error as fast as possible

by an FCS. If recognized and properly harnessed, the new

Generation X personalities will be the best agents for change

and adoption of Skinny Finance. Here is what to expect from this

generation of administrators.

Personal & General Characteristics:

- Generation X has more formal education than that of the Boomer Generation.
- The new generation is more culturally diverse than previous generations
- Generation X is more integrated into a service economy than generations prior.
- The Generation X is more technologically adept. (Arriola 2005)

Workplace Characteristics:
- Eliminate the task
- Self Reliance
- Want structure and direction
- Skeptical
(Hammill, 2005)

Leadership Style:
- Everyone is the same
- Challenge others
- Ask Why (Pay special attention to this one.)
(Hammill, 2005)

According to some research, the Baby Boomer generation before the Generation X, has not made it a priority to teach leadership skills to the new generation of leaders.

> "The problem posed by the upcoming generational changing of the guard is that the generation in line to succeed the Boomers, the Gen X-ers, has not been equipped with the leadership skills and knowledge needed to assume the responsibility being passed on to it. Due to generational differences, the Baby Boomers have not been good about sharing their knowledge and experience, and Generation X has not been good about tapping into it." (Gilburg, 2007)

This admonition cautions that the leaders of today need to take a proactive role in the leadership development of their successor generation. Since the Generation X leaders respond to and expect feedback to their work (Hammill, 2005) it should be a simple objective to formally introduce the concepts of leadership and senior administration.

> "[T]his generation expects immediate and ongoing feedback, and is equally comfortable giving feedback to others." (Thielfoldt and Scheef, 2004)

Perhaps I had it easy. By beginning my career at a young age, I had access to two mentor generations: the Baby Boomer Generation and the Traditionalists. During my experiences, I learned that the more senior generation, the Traditionalists, tend

to be more willing to provide direct and formal feedback and

make a conscious effort to train the next generation. The Baby

Boomers, the largest generation in the country's history, seems

to be leaving the training of new leaders to a self-directed

program. While this is not a concerted effort by the Baby

Boomers, it is the <u>de facto</u> method of training. And in the

absence of direction, Generation X tends to self-direct.

What are the consequences for Skinny Finance? In the

best of all worlds, the Generation X leaders with their integration

of technology and a proclivity to ask "why," will self-direct

themselves to a naturally Skinny Finance. That is, they have the

key cultural elements for producing a lean, efficient Finance

Department. They are quick to adopt new technologies to solve

everyday problems and they question the purposes behind

business activities. (Hammill, 2005)

The key asset offered by Generation X in making a

smooth transition to Skinny Finance, is that, according to

Hammill, the Generation X seeks direction. They want the formal

and informal training. As the senior administrators, you might want to jump for joy. Here is a very capable generation who is seeking direction and their natural tendency is to produce Skinny Finance. Remember the Zebra story above? The reason a bookstore accountant stepped forward to lead the inventory project may have been that she was a Generation X-er. She was culturally programmed to desire change. Consequently, is it any wonder that the Computer Services Department quickly adopted her project? They were all Generation X as well.

Our generation demands results. It is not sufficient to simply talk a good political game, make all the right contacts and then leave implementation for the next person. People of the newer generation are typically doers. During accreditation visits of other educational institutions, I have been known to say: "Planning to Plan is not a plan." What I mean by that quip is that developing a timeline or a meeting schedule or even configuring a committee is not an actual plan. Further, the plan, in and of itself, is worthless unless there is implementation. This is a common value shared among my colleagues of this generation. Unless we hold a product in our hands or we see a service delivered, there is no value in simply planning to do something.

The Point: Always asking why, the Generation X members are great advocates for change to a Skinny Finance. They often need, however, the leadership development that has typically been passed from generation to generation but is currently not taking place.

Buffering

In a Southern California School District, an acquaintance of mine was implementing his own form of Skinny Finance. The change resulted in the issuance of credit cards to the high level administrators. This is a common way to show you trust your budget managers that you trust their decision-making abilities. By the time the credit card expenditure is made and receipts are submitted to the Department of Finance, it is too late for staff to stop the transaction. This is part of the cultural change called for by Skinny Finance. We trust budget managers to manage.

So this manager received his district credit card and began managing his program without benefit of the pre-approval, approval and Über-approval system to which his district formerly adhered. As he operated his program, he came upon the opportunity to take a retreat with his staff. Under the Board Policies, there was no problem with this. The problem came when he submitted his credit card receipts including several hundreds of dollars in restaurant bills. They included a lot of alcohol. This was a violation of Board Policy. He was admonished and sent back to duty with instructions to not purchase alcohol on his district credit card.

The second time he purchased alcohol with his district credit card, he explained the dilemma he had. He told me a couple of years after, that he was in the restaurant and had ordered drinks. After he and his party finished, he realized he only had the district credit card. Now I can think of many solutions to this dilemma that do not involve purchasing alcohol on the district credit card, again. He did not make such a judgment. His expenditure was, once again, inappropriate. He was fired.

This Skinny Book about Skinny Finance makes a bold proposition to change the culture of the Department of Finance to be one that is customer-oriented, lean and process-based. It proposes to encourage risk-taking by the Department of Finance while they leave the historically centralized decision-making process and decentralize the system of expenditure approvals. The inference from the book may be that one simply walks into the Department of Finance, circles the day on the calendar and

declares "This is the date we change philosophy." As you can

imagine, it is not that simple. The concept of buffering is

intended to aid in implementation of Skinny Finance.

There are fifteen definitions of "buffer" located at

www.dictionary.com. Perhaps the most appropriate definition for

the purposes discussed in this book is:

> "[A] person or thing that shields and protects
> against annoyance, harm, hostile forces, etc., or
> that lessens the impact of a shock or reversal."
> (Dictionary, 2008)

During the process of making your Department of

Finance "Skinny," best results will be achieved when a system of

buffers is used. For instance, while the department rearranges

work tasks and assignments, it will be helpful if the priorities are

not disrupted. An effective buffer in this case would prevent the

demands of *ad hoc* report requirements that may arrive from the

Board or other administrators. It is the responsibility of the senior

administrators to serve the needs of these clients while the

Department of Finance establishes its new priorities and a new

culture.

Buffering can also be used effectively to change the mindset of the program and budget managers. My acquaintance described above would have been well-served by changing his mindset with respect to the credit cards and alcohol. Under Skinny Finance, the program managers will be operating without the benefit of the "Last Line of Defense." Many program managers will welcome this change that gives them real control over their budgets. However, as the Department of Finance releases control of the test for "appropriateness," the budget managers need to step up and understand that this audit is now truly under their control.

Be careful what you wish for, you might get it. I have heard for two decades that program managers want real control over their budgets. However, I have seen a minority of managers who do not actually want the responsibility of managing the "appropriateness" of the expenditures. I assure you these are the small minority. But the senior administrators need to commit to Skinny Finance and assure the Department of Finance is buffered from the inevitable inappropriate expenditure.

The logic of this Organizational Development is simple. The program managers are fully capable leaders who run complex instructional programs. Since they have been hired to manage a budget, let them manage. By looking at the process of expenditure authorization and avoiding the tedium of transaction-based analysis, Skinny Finance trusts the managers to actually manage their budgets. The senior administrators need to communicate the new expectation to the constituent groups and be ready to support Skinny Finance when the inevitable happens. Inappropriate expenditures will occur. And they already do occur. The senior administrator support may require reeducation of the program managers as they are now the only "line of defense" for inappropriate expenditures.

The Point: Under Skinny Finance senior administrators need to assume a role of buffer for the Department of Finance.

Information Technology

As far as I am concerned Technology and Finance Departments should be the closest of friends in education. In every institution I have worked, I have found a technology staff that is eager to try new things and to solve my departments' challenges. They are non-territorial and easily reached. The Finance Department was created to safeguard assets and help the institution to conduct business. The biggest difference between the Finance and Technology cultures is that Finance seeks new ideas but is risk averse. Technology staff seeks new ideas and will take a risk. Finance lives in a culture of rules and boundaries and Technology lives in a world that challenges boundaries and reduces rules to a set of conditions.

When I was Director of Finance and Technology at Escondido Union High School District, the State of California had just started the Digital High School Grants. Millions of dollars were to be immediately pumped into technology in public schools and I had one foot in each door: technology and finance. It was a culture shock to get the two departments together. On the one hand, I had finance staff that knew the grant rules forward and backward. On the other hand, my technology staff knew the state of the art and wanted to implement the most technology for the students, faculty and staff. Finance moved cautiously and Technology moved quickly. Finance staff had grown children the age of the technology staff. The contrasts could continue for pages.

But ultimately we got the two departments together to meet each other and to discuss the Digital High School Grants. Once each was properly motivated and had a clear role, everyone became eager to participate. I explained to Finance that Technology needed their attention to make sure they did not spend too much time developing budgets. I explained to Technology that Finance needed upgraded systems to accommodate more demanding financial reporting requirements. They needed each other. But sometimes a cultural barrier can keep two parties apart despite their interdependence.

If you are so blessed as to work with both Technology and Finance, you will find a wonderful world of precise planning and budgeting (Finance) and a culture of challenging barriers and boundaries (Technology). When they work together, Finance gets skinny very quickly. The biggest challenges of administering the two together are:

1.   Don't let the departments' differences divide them from a common purpose.
2.   Create an expectation in which they ask each other for help.

From managing the Technology Department, I learned that the biggest challenge to new system implementation or enhancement stems from the fact that the Technology Department is not asked or consulted by the people who need their help. Please ask them. The worst thing that can happen is that they will not find an immediate solution to your problem. Similarly, the Finance Department is waiting to be asked for help in all business matters; ask them. Both departments tend to be very helpful people who just need to know who needs assistance.

The Point: Encourage Finance and Technology to work together and look for the similarities between the two cultures.

In Parting

The profession of education is bifurcated between instruction and business services. While the instructors are encouraged to and rewarded for thinking in new ways and eliminating boundaries and convention, the Department of Finance is rewarded for conservation and elimination of risk. This difference is often made more pronounced when instruction and finance collaborate on projects. There is a culture shock. On the one hand, the instructors have a culture that challenges convention and on the other finance creates and reinforces convention.

It is neither feasible nor desired to eliminate all rules of finance. We still need to protect the assets of the district. However, by challenging our finance departments to decentralize control of program budgets, an educational institution will be more efficient and will better meet the needs of the client departments. But this model relies heavily upon support from the senior administrators and Board. It is not sufficient to merely buffer the workload of the Department of Finance and hope for the best. We must also support a culture of innovation and creativity.

Implementation of Skinny Finance presents a context in which administrators manage the expectations of the institution. This new context requires culture rich in support of people while strictly critiquing financial systems. Purchasing and financing become lean in their impact on the program managers but robust in the analysis of the processes by which those services are delivered.

The Skinny Finance model assumes that program managers are more knowledgeable about program needs than the Department of Finance and creates an expectation that the managers will execute the business functions conforming to the Strategic Plans of the institution. The expectation that finance is the "last line of defense" for inappropriate expenditures disappears and the emergent expectation is that the program administrators manage their own budgets.

This condition of authority requires the responsibility of the program managers become explicit and central to the success of the institution. The Department of Finance moves away from the transactional analysis that leads to tedious questioning of the program budgets and expenditures and toward a process of system evaluation.

Sticking true to my heritage as a Generation X-er, I am always in search of "why." Why do we do the things we do? And I ask "how." How can we provide better services? How can we provide the same level of service with fewer resources?

In the world of education, the finance employees are not "Pilots." But like the Air Force example above, we are in the business of keeping the planes flying. And since we work in a profession of financial scarcity, we need to always work to deliver more services with fewer resources. In education, the finances are scarce but the innovation, creativity and ingenuity of our staff are abundant. We simply need to create a culture that supports and encourages the implementation of the models we can design. We need a culture of risk-taking.

This change in culture will be easier for some educational institutions than for others. To aid the transition to a Skinny Finance, a web resource has been established to focus resources for the administrators who want to investigate this new culture: www.SkinnyAdmin.com. This web site chronicles the stories of educational administration; we would love to publish your experiences.

The site also provides a set of tools that help make the transition to Skinny Finance. For example, the site offers a sophisticated web survey tool that can be used to assess the culture and guide the institution toward a commonly shared goal. In addition, the site will present to you a list of professionals who support Skinny Finance through, accounting, legal and information technology resources.

Please research this site and you will find other institutions on the same journey – to Skinny Finance.

www.SkinnyAdmin.com

It is important during this review of Skinny Finance that you communicate with your staff and the campus communities.

By researching the anecdotes of other institutions, you will see the variety of cultures and the range of solutions available to help your institution through its cultural transformation to Skinny Finance.

The Point: Communicate, communicate, communicate. Be quick to listen to all the parties affected by Skinny Finance, which should be all campus communities.

References

Arriola, Fernando. 2005. Characteristics of Generation X, Denver, Colorado. City of Denver. Available at www.denvergov.org/Portals/229/documents/Characteristi cs%20of%20Gen%20X.ppt, Internet. Accessed April 18, 2008.

Dictionary. 2008. Definition of "Buffer." Available at: http://dictionary.reference.com/browse/buffer Internet. Accessed April 19, 2008.

Gilburg, Deborah. 2007. Generation X: Stepping Up to the Leadership Plate: How to leverage the mind-share of retiring Baby Boomers to advance your career. CIO.com. January 31, 2007. Available at: http://www.cio.com/article/28475. Internet. Accessed January 20, 2008.

Hammill, Greg. 2005. Mixing and Managing Four Generations of Employees. Denver, Colorado. FDU Magazine Online. Available at http://www.fdu.edu/newspubs/magazine/05ws/generation s.htm. Internet. Accessed April 1, 2008.

Howell, G.H. and G. Ballard (1998), "Implementing Lean Construction: Understanding and Action." Proceedings of the 6th Annual Conference of the International Group for Lean Construction, Guaruja, Brazil. Available at www.iglc.net.

Johnson, Wayne C. 1998. Defeating Proposition 223: how opponents of the "95/5" school funding initiative dramatically turned around public opinion to beat it 55-45. Internet. Available at http://findarticles.com/p/articles/mi_m2519/is_n10_v19/ai _21227951/pg_1. Accessed April 18, 2008.

Li, Yaling. 2003. Fiscal Closing June 30, 2003. Berkeley, California. Internet. Available at http://generalaccounting.berkeley.edu/FiscalClose/Close Letter-03.htm. Accessed April 4, 2008.

Stephens, Jon C. 1998. Analysis of 95/5 Initiative for Escondido Union High School District. Escondido, California: Escondido Union High School District.

Thielfoldt, Diane and Scheef, Devon. 2004. Generation X and The Millennials: What You Need to Know About Mentoring the New Generations. August 2004. Law Practice Today. Internet. Available at http http://www.abanet.org/lpm/lpt/articles/mgt08044.html. Accessed March 4, 2008.

About the Author

Jon C. Stephens earned his Doctorate in Education from the University of La Verne in 2008, MBA in Financial Management from National University in San Diego and a BA in Economics at the University of California, San Diego.

Over the past twenty years, Dr. Stephens has worked in both K-12 and Community Colleges in Administrative and Instructional positions. He currently serves as the Vice President of Business Services at San Joaquin Delta College in Stockton, California. From 2005 to 2008 he served as Senior Director at BRJ & Associates, a consultant to California public schools and colleges. He served Lake Tahoe Community

College as Vice President of Business Services from 1999 to 2005. In addition he has served the educational communities at: Escondido Union Elementary School District, MiraCosta Community College and Escondido Union High School District. Dr. Stephens has taught community college courses in: Public Speaking and Computer and Information Sciences.

Dr. Stephens has published articles in the <u>CASBO Journal of School Business Management</u> regarding community college investment policies and enrollment projection. Other literary works include "In a Box," a study of the enrollment fee policy of the California Community Colleges.

You can find "In a Box" published by VDM Publishing at: www.Amazon.com.